VOLUME 18

SING WITH THE CHOIR
AUDIO INCLUDED

Disney SONGS

T0081872

Audio Access Included

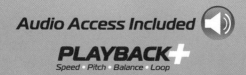
PLAYBACK+
Speed • Pitch • Balance • Loop

To access audio visit:
www.halleonard.com/mylibrary

Enter Code
8380-1675-5238-5826

ISBN 978-1-5400-5970-3

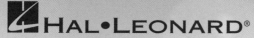
HAL•LEONARD®

Visit Hal Leonard Online at
www.halleonard.com

Contact us:
Hal Leonard
7777 West Bluemound Road
Milwaukee, WI 53213
Email: info@halleonard.com

In Europe, contact:
Hal Leonard Europe Limited
42 Wigmore Street
Marylebone, London, W1U 2RN
Email: info@halleonardeurope.com

In Australia, contact:
Hal Leonard Australia Pty. Ltd.
4 Lentara Court
Cheltenham, Victoria, 3192 Australia
Email: info@halleonard.com.au

CONTENTS

From HERCULES

Go the Distance

Arranged by
JOHN LEAVITT

Music by ALAN MENKEN
Lyrics by DAVID ZIPPEL

he - ro's strength is meas - ured by his heart.
Sop. only — Oo, — Alto only — oo, —
Bass only — Ten. only —

28

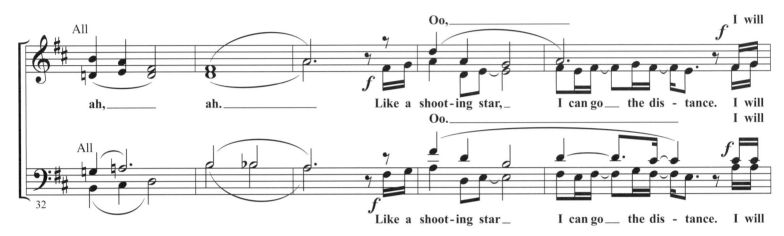

All ah, — ah. — Like a shoot-ing star, — I can go — the dis - tance. I will
Oo, — I will
Oo. — I will
All Like a shoot-ing star — I can go — the dis - tance. I will

32

I don't care how far. —
search the world. — I will face — its harms. I don't care how far. —

37

till I
I can go the dis - tance till I find my he - ro's wel-come wait - ing in — your
I can go the dis - tance till I

40

Broadly (♩ = ca. 70)

rit. *tenuto* *a tempo*
div.
arms, in your arms!
tenuto *a tempo*
rit.

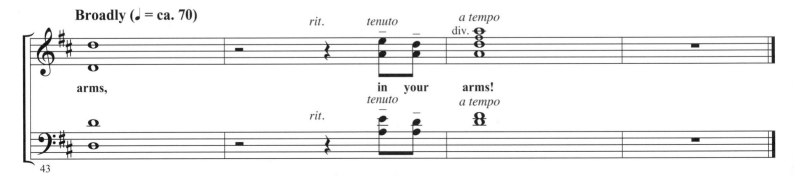

43

From FROZEN

Let It Go

Arranged by
MAC HUFF

Music and Lyrics by
KRISTEN ANDERSON-LOPEZ
and ROBERT LOPEZ

8

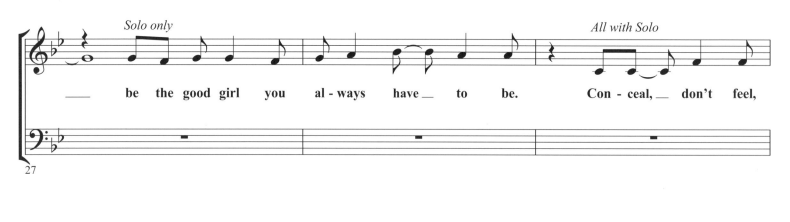

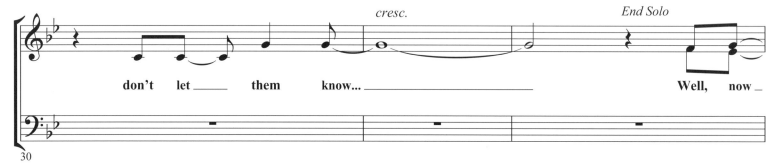

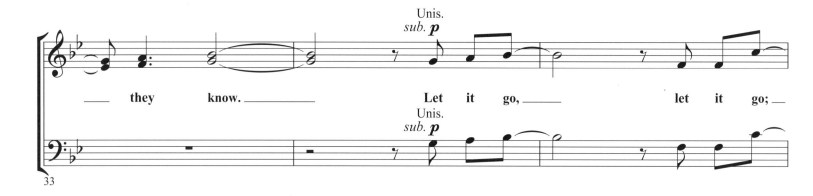

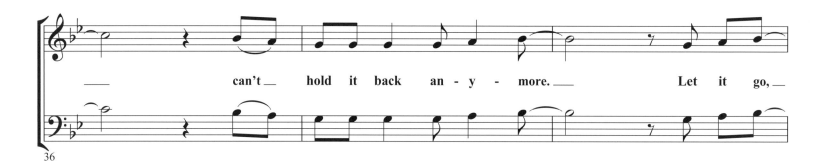

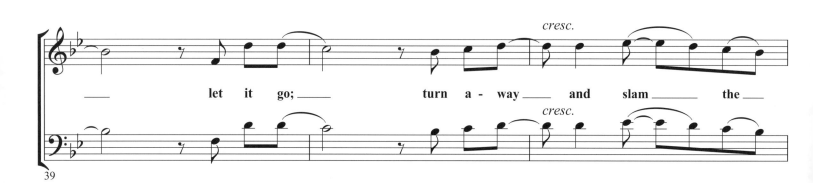

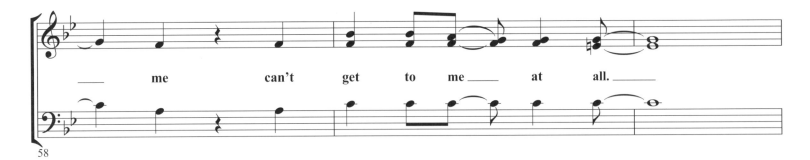

me can't get to me ___ at all. ___

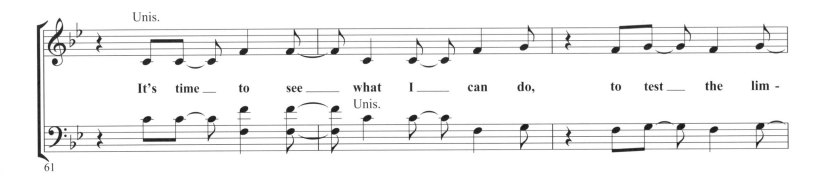

Unis.

It's time ___ to see ___ what I ___ can do, to test ___ the lim -

Unis.

cresc.

- its and ___ break through. ___ No right, ___ no wrong, ___ no rules ___ for me; ___

cresc.

I'm free! _____ *f* Let it go, ___ let it go; ___

f

Unis.

I am one with the wind and sky. ___ Let it go, ___

Unis.

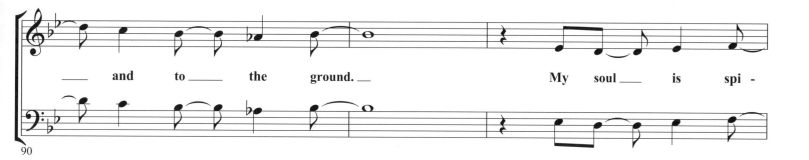

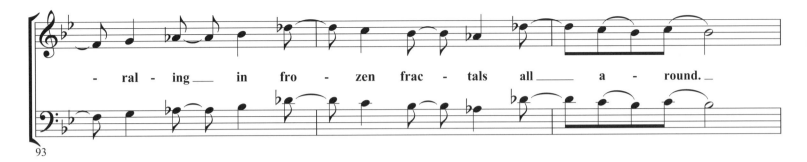

-ral - ing __ in fro - zen frac - tals all __ a - round. __

93

And one __ thought crys - tal - liz - es like __ an i - cy blast: __

96

I'm nev - er go - ing back; __ the

99

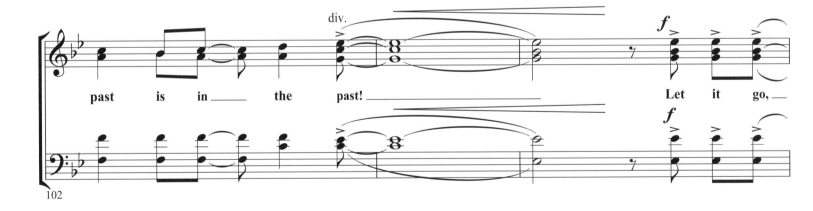

past is in __ the past! _____ Let it go, __

102

__ let it go, __ and I'll rise __ like the break __ of dawn. __

105

Let it go, _____ let it go; _____ that per -

- fect girl _____ is _____ gone. _____ Here _____ I _____ stand _____

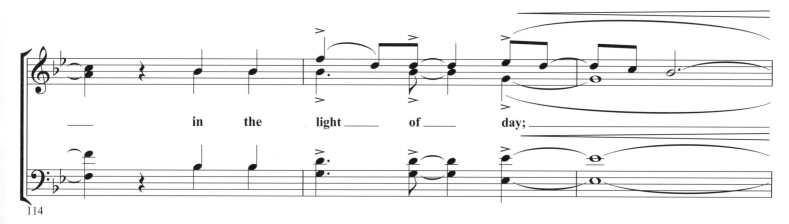

_____ in the light _____ of _____ day; _____

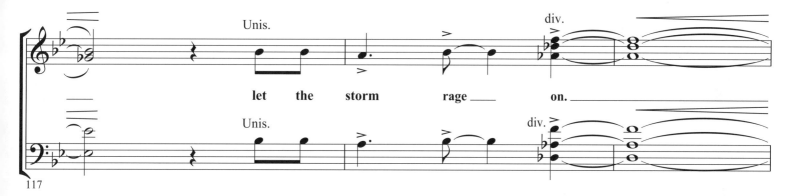

let the storm rage _____ on. _____

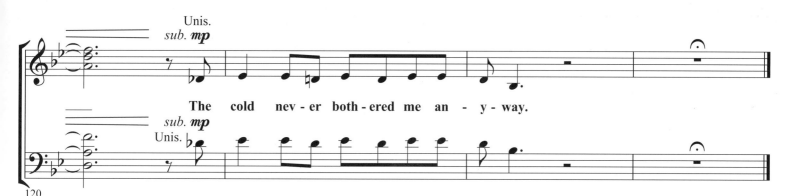

The cold nev - er both - ered me an - y - way.

From MOANA

How Far I'll Go

Arranged by
ED LOJESKI

Words and Music by
LIN-MANUEL MIRANDA

From TANGLED

I See the Light

Arranged by
MAC HUFF

Music by ALAN MENKEN
Lyrics by GLENN SLATER

20

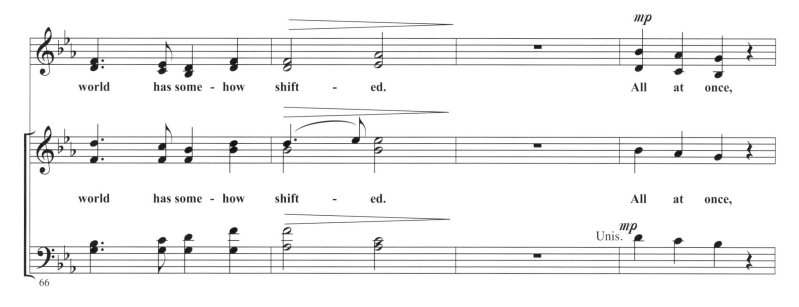

world has some - how shift - ed.   All   at   once,

world has some - how shift - ed.   All   at   once,

Unis.

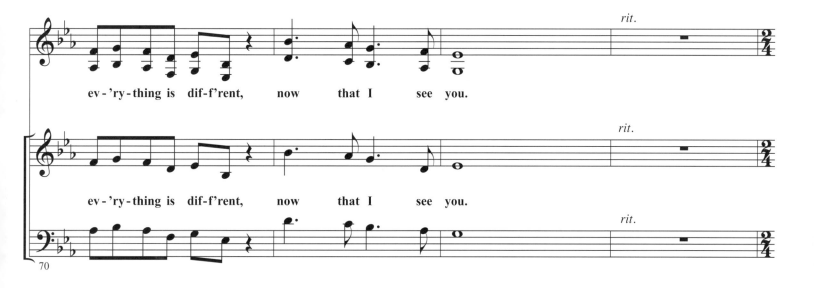

ev - 'ry-thing is dif-f'rent,   now   that I   see you.

ev - 'ry-thing is dif-f'rent,   now   that I   see you.

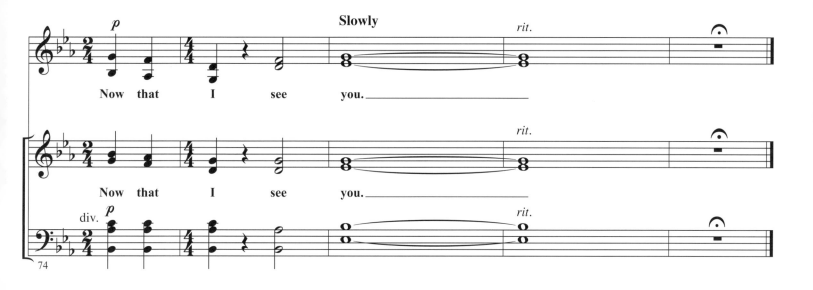

Now   that   I   see   you._____

Now   that   I   see   you._____

div.

From MARY POPPINS RETURNS

Nowhere to Go But Up

Arranged by
ROGER EMERSON

Music by MARC SHAIMAN
Lyrics by SCOTT WITTMAN
and MARC SHAIMAN

24

Solo *mf*

Just one day at the fair has me waltz - ing on air! And there's

end Solo

no - where to go but up. Now my

Piu mosso (♩ = ca. 168)

heart is so light that I think I just might start

cresc. poco a poco

feed - ing the birds, and then go fly a kite! With your

cresc. poco a poco

head in a cloud on - ly laugh - ter's al - lowed, and there's

no - where to go but up.

no - where to go but up. As you

fly o - ver town it gets hard - er to frown, and we'll

all hit the heights if we nev - er look down. Let the

past take a bow: the for - ev - er is now. And there's no - where to

go but up. Up! There's no - where to go but

up!

From MARY POPPINS RETURNS

The Place Where Lost Things Go

Arranged by
MAC HUFF

Music by MARC SHAIMAN
Lyrics by SCOTT WITTMAN
and MARC SHAIMAN

gone for good, you feared, they're all a - round you still, though they've

dis - ap - peared. Noth - ing's real - ly left,_____ or

poco rit. lost with - out a trace. Noth - ing's gone for - ev - er, on - ly

Unis. *mp* *a tempo* out of place. So may - be now the dish and my best spoon are

Unis. play - ing hide and seek just be - hind the moon, *cresc.* wait - ing there un - til it's

where you need her touch and lov - ing gaze, "gone, but not for - got - ten," is the per - fect phrase. Smil - ing from a star that she makes glow, trust she's al - ways there, watch - ing as you grow. Find her in the place where the lost things go. Oo.

From COCO

Remember Me
(Ernesto de la Cruz)

Arranged by
ROGER EMERSON

Words and Music by
KRISTEN ANDERSON-LOPEZ
and ROBERT LOPEZ

Know that I'm with you the on - ly way that I can be.

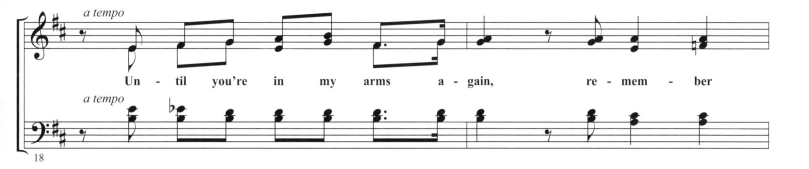

Un - til you're in my arms a - gain, re - mem - ber

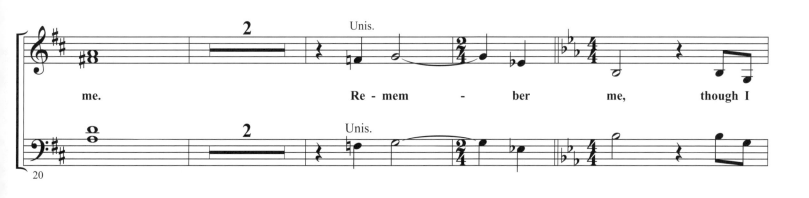

me.   Re - mem - ber   me,   though I

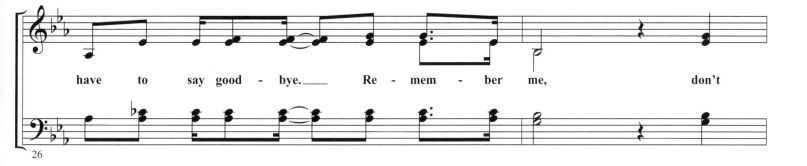

have to say good - bye.____ Re - mem - ber me,   don't

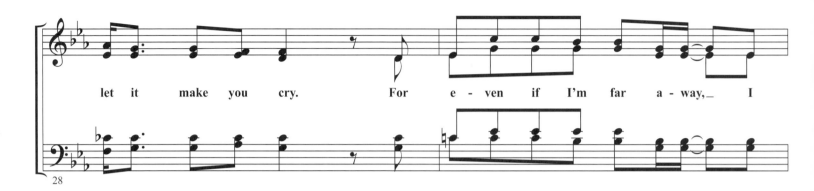

let it make you cry. For e - ven if I'm far a - way,_ I

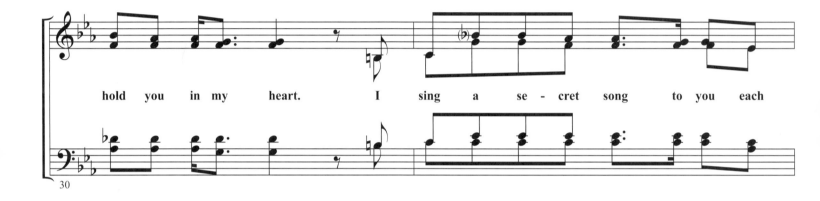

hold you in my heart. I sing a se - cret song to you each

night we are a - part. Re - mem - - ber me, though I
Re - mem - - ber me. Re - mem - ber

have to trav - el far.__ Re - mem - ber me each time you
me. Re - mem - ber

hear   a   sad   gui - tar.   Know   that   I'm   with   you   the   on - ly

me.

way   that   I   can   be._____   Un - til   you're   in   my   arms   a -

gain,   re - mem - ber   me,   re -

re - mem - ber   me._____

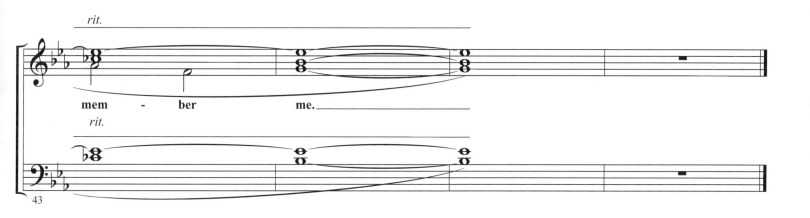

mem - ber   me._____

From MOANA

We Know the Way

Arranged by
ROGER EMERSON

Music by OPETAIA FOA'I
Lyrics by OPETAIA FOA'I and
LIN-MANUEL MIRANDA

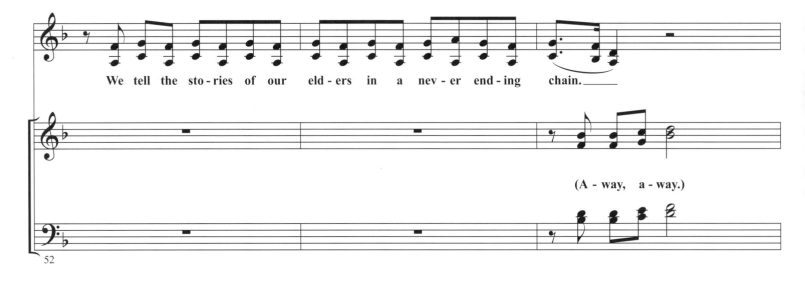

We tell the sto- ries of our eld- ers in a nev- er end- ing chain.

(A - way, a - way.)

Unis.

Te fen- ua te mal- i- e. Na- e ko ha- ki- li- a. We know the way!

Te fen- ua te mal- i- e. Na- e ko ha- ki- li- a. We know the way!

div.

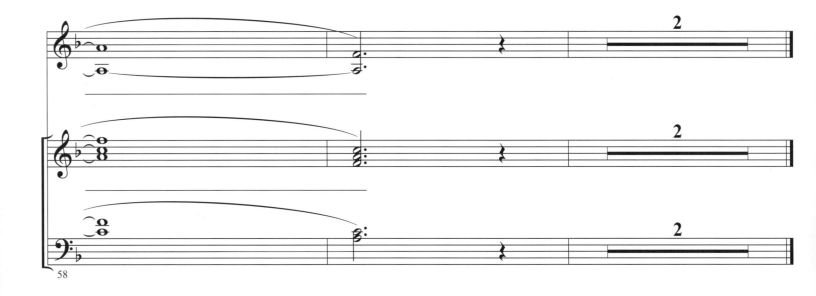